There's An Old Sout

The Wit and Wisdom of Dan May

Dan May, 1898 – 1982

Compiled by William May Stern

Foreword by Robert K. Massie

Dedication

I REMEMBER STANDING in the library at The Temple in Nashville. The day was December 20, 1982. The funeral service for my grandpa had just ended, and I was in the receiving line with the rest of my family. The service had been standing-room-only. Not surprisingly, many of Nashville's leading citizens had come. When they passed through the receiving line, they all said the thoughtful things that a 21-year-old grandson would expect to hear. Then an elderly, stooped man stopped in front of me. His coat and tie were frayed, but clean. He said he wanted to tell me about my grandpa. And he did.

He told me he had worked for 40 years for my grandpa at the May Hosiery Mills, and that my grandpa had always treated him with dignity and respect. He said he'd never met a white man like that before. He said my grandpa could be hard on people, but was always fair and often generous, and that he could be funny, but was also awfully smart. He told me that even though he was old and didn't get out much anymore, he'd gotten his son to drive him out to the Jewish church today because he thought Mr. Dan's grandchildren should know what kind of man he was. He said I should be proud of my grandpa because there will never be another one like him. And then he said that Dan May was the finest man he'd ever known.

Up until then, I had been reasonably composed. But as he moved on down the receiving line, I was fighting back the tears. I never found out who that black man was. A few years later, I became a writer. At some point, I resolved that my children and grandchildren should know what kind of man my grandpa was. So I started collecting his stories. This book is for them – Dan May's descendants who will never have the chance to know him as I did.

W.M.S.

∽ Table of Contents ∽

~ Foreword ~

WHEN I WAS A BOY growing up in Nashville, Tennessee in the 1940s, Dan May was my good friend's father. To Dan, I suppose, I began as one of the tribe of nameless boys who trooped through his front door and followed his son up the stairs. Nevertheless, for me, Dan was different from other fathers. For one thing, he was home before the end of the afternoon; because he went to work early, he was back in his house not long after we were out of school. So there he was, reading a book or newspaper in his living room, subject to encounter. "You're Molly Todd's boys," he said, looking up from his page when he first saw me and my brother, Kim. "She's a fine woman, but of course her politics are dead wrong." (My mother, who was active in local politics and civic organizations, was – and at 89 remains – an indomitable Democrat; Dan was a lifelong Republican.)

Dan, almost from the beginning, took me seriously. I believed in Franklin D. Roosevelt, the New Deal, TVA, the United Nations, Harry Truman, and labor unions. Dan, as I recall, was down on all the items on this list. But he did not scoff or harumph and walk away. Instead, he explained how business worked, how capitalism worked, how the economy worked, and how, in his view, this contributed not just to individual wealth and personal freedom, but to the greatest good for the greatest number. I listened hard and learned much, and if I did not embrace all of his views, at least I began to question some of my own. To this day, my political opinions go down the middle, somewhere between the unshakable Republicanism of Dan May and the fervent Democratic liberalism of Molly Todd.

Dan's talk was peppered with humor: oneliners, puns, double entendres. Some were original, some borrowed; Dan's special skill was in precisely matching the joke to the tale he was telling or the point he was trying to make. In my mind's eye, I see him clearly: dark face, intense brown eyes, a bright smile, rapid-fire voice with a slight lisp which, as with Winston Churchill, made his speech distinctive so that you listened closely.

Jokes bubbled out of him. He knew, as they say, "a million of 'em." Somewhere under his lid, he kept a joke for every occasion and when the occasion presented itself, he pounced unstoppably. Dorothy May, married to Dan for 50 years, must have heard them all, but she never complained. Sometimes, she laughed; more often she patiently shook her head with a small, enigmatic smile, perhaps in response to the joke, perhaps in recognition of the aptness of its selection for the moment at hand, perhaps at the folly of humankind – or perhaps in wonder at the inexhaustible humor of her inexhaustible husband.

Dan's humor had an edge. It was Jewish humor; it drew on skepticism, irony, even cynicism. Dan deflated bombast in people, ideas, and institutions. It was self-deprecating, thereby earning the right to deprecate others. I felt a sting when Dan once told me "the only time the words 'Jesus Christ' are pronounced with fervor in an Episcopal church is when the janitor falls down the stairs." My grandfather was (and my son now is) an Episcopal minister and I remember feeling that Dan was trespassing unfairly. The next minute, though, Dan would be telling a story about a rabbi who lusted after his secretary, voted Democratic and craved bacon.

To describe Dan May's humor as Jewish is insufficient; it was Southern Jewish. Dan spent his life in Nashville and during this three-quarters of a century, Nashville was compartmented into separate worlds: white and black, Jewish and Christian. Dan was a liberal before it was fashionable; in all his immense repertoire, if he had black jokes, I never remember hearing them. Certainly, he felt the dividing line between Jews and Christians – in Nashville society, a Christian lunched with a Jew, but rarely invited him home to dinner. Jewish boys and Christian girls did not date. Country clubs, fraternities, sororities, law firms and group medical practices were firmly segregated by religion. Dan bumped against these invisible lines all his life, pretending not to notice or not to care. Humor was his sword and shield. Not invited to dinner? Am I supposed to be unhappy? Do you know what the WASP mama said to the little Jewish boy when he asked if he could stay to dinner...?

Many of Dan May's jokes and stories have worked their way into my own more limited repertoire where they hide in the shadows, waiting to be triggered by association. Here are two of my favorites which Willy Stern, for all his remarkable thoroughness, has missed:

– *"There are always four versions of any speech I give," Dan once told me. "The first is the speech I plan to give. The second is the speech I actually give. The third is the speech I wish I had given when I get home and think about it. And the fourth is the speech I read about in* **The Tennessean** *the next morning."*

– *Dan May and his close friend Vanderbilt Chancellor Harvie Branscomb die at the same time and arrive together at the Pearly Gates. St. Peter, handing out room assignments, says that Paradise is crowded and new arrivals will have to double up. They go off to the dormitory where Dan finds that his bedmate is a hideous crone while Branscomb discovers that he is sharing a bed with Bo Derek. "I'm sorry, Mr. May," St. Peter says, "but here we are handing out divine justice and we both know that your life was filled with sins." "True," says Dan, "but certainly I was no worse than Branscomb and look who you've put him with!" "Ah yes," St. Peter says, "but here the problem is with Miss Derek. On earth she behaved every bit as sinfully as you did."*

No one laughed harder at this story than Harvie Branscomb.

Robert K. Massie
Irvington, New York

Dan May had an old copy of *The Oxford Dictionary of Quotations*. The only three passages he marked in the book follow:

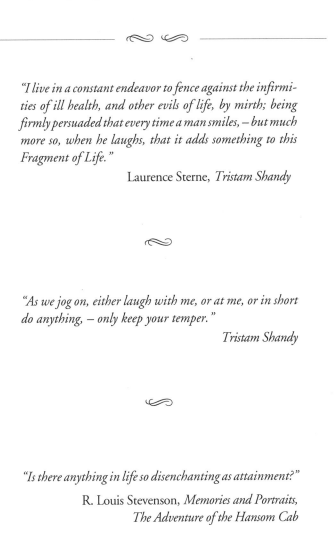

"I live in a constant endeavor to fence against the infirmities of ill health, and other evils of life, by mirth; being firmly persuaded that every time a man smiles, – but much more so, when he laughs, that it adds something to this Fragment of Life."

Laurence Sterne, *Tristam Shandy*

"As we jog on, either laugh with me, or at me, or in short do anything, – only keep your temper."

Tristam Shandy

"Is there anything in life so disenchanting as attainment?"

R. Louis Stevenson, *Memories and Portraits,*
The Adventure of the Hansom Cab

~1~

Families & Relationships

A Man Who Didn't Make the Same Mistake Once

"D
efinition of a bachelor: A man who didn't make the same mistake once.

Whenever a husband or wife is murdered by his or her spouse, you never have to look for a motive.

Choosing mates wisely is the best prevention of divorce.

Viewing a total eclipse of the sun was the most exciting 90 seconds I've ever had with my clothes on.

I'll start carrying around photos of my grandchildren as soon as they start carrying around photos of me.

Advice to first-time fathers: When your wife brings the baby home, offer to hold it, then drop it. It won't hurt the baby a bit, and your wife will never ask you to do anything with the baby again.

I always forget it. What's the word that means that you can only be married to one person? Monotony?

Misers are only good for one thing – ancestors.

Then there was the story of the fellow who received a letter from another fellow that read, "I resent your running around with my wife when I am out of the city. Come to my office tomorrow at 10 a.m."

Fellow #1 replied, "I received your circular letter, but I cannot attend the meeting. I'll go along with what all the other fellows decide."

What's the difference between a bachelor woman and an old maid? A bachelor woman has never been married. An old maid has never been married ... or anything!

Two elderly gentlemen were at a funeral at a cemetery outside of Nashville. Said one, "It hardly pays to go back to town."

I've got more friends out here than I do downtown.

... in his 70s, at a funeral.

I already have two of everything, and I don't want three of anything.

... discouraging gift-givers at birthday time.

Advice to young women: Marry someone who is smart, who is healthy, and who has a pleasant disposition.

Don't ever get married thinking you can change your partner's personality.

Then there was the story about the fellow who was out cutting his grass one day in a ritzy Nashville suburb. The fellow had gotten married several years before to a very rich lady. It was a scalding hot summer afternoon, and the fellow had taken his shirt off.

A policeman happened by and said, "You shouldn't be out here without your shirt on. What would people think if your wife was out here cutting the grass without her shirt on?"

The fellow replied, "They'd be sure I married her for her money!"

If the woman you fall in love with happens to be rich, don't hold it against her.

A long time ago I discovered that you never anger a father by complimenting his children.

Children hear nothing you say, but notice everything you do.

Be a model to your children, not a critic.

Rule #1 in how to handle your children: Don't interfere with their lives.

The best parents don't need the benefit of the many How-To-Raise-Children books. They use the most worthwhile method: Example and expectancy.

The little boy was standing on the corner. He was crying and crying. A man came up to the boy and asked, "What's the matter?"

"My mother and father are arguing all the time," he replied.

"Who is your father?" the fellow inquired.

"That's what they're arguing about!"

There's one infallible method for determining if a couple eating together in a restaurant is married. If they're talking to each other, they aren't married.

Anyone who marries for money earns every penny of it. The pay is good, but the hours are long.

Then there's the story of the Jewish lady who gave her husband two neckties for his birthday. The next day he came down to breakfast, proudly wearing one of his new ties."I knew it," she said. "I knew you didn't like the other one."

There is one advantage we have in the country over the city; you can tell when you become an elderly gentleman — you are no longer asked to tote but become an honorary pallbearer.

You become 75 only once. That's true for 76 and 74, but not true for 39.

I always doubt the validity of the claim that divorce is better than having a loveless home, for if there was ever real love between the pair, it can be restored if the policy of "forgive and forget" is applied. Even more than once or twice. Maybe daily!

I advise caution against getting too romantically involved at a young age. As George Washington said, beware entangling alliances.

... paraphrasing Washington's Farewell Address in 1796, when the first president stated, "'Tis our true policy to stay clear of permanent alliance, with any portion of the foreign world."

Then there was the lady whose husband asked her to go to Cox Department Store to buy a seersucker suit, but she got confused and ended up at Sears.

Samuel Johnson was right when he said that second marriages represent "the triumph of hope over experience."

My neighbor once said to her husband in my presence, "When one of us dies, I'll move to New York tomorrow."

I can't describe a pretty girl, but I know one when I see one.

They used to say you can't take it with you, but now they've fixed it so you can't leave it behind.

... after a new law was passed that increased inheritance taxes.

There is a great difference between love, libido and marriage. The first two are normal human and animal impulses and drives; marriage is a legal and social device. Even with people of the same background and economic groups, with the same traditions, the problems are manifold. Few, if any, can go through life without insurmountable problems developing. (Of course, bachelors have worse problems.)

Then there was the married woman who tried unsuccessfully for years to have children, and decided to visit a fertility doctor. After the examination, the doctor said he could find nothing wrong with her, and suggested he check out her husband.

"There's no use doing that," she replied. "You see, I haven't been depending on him entirely."

When my good friend Bernard "Bud" Fensterwald married a woman named Betsy Vosberry, I couldn't attend the wedding, but sent a telegram: "Tis spring, the Vosberrys are in bud, and vice-versa."

2

Health & Medicine

Shoot Your Grandfather Before You're Born

"I was Dan's doctor. He had an affectionate slogan for me: 'If you're tired of living, see Riven.' He was a well-known after-dinner speaker. Once he was asked to address the Brotherhood meeting of the West End Presbyterian Church. He asked me if I cared to come along and hear what he had to say.

"He started his talk, and said, 'You know, I always travel with my doctor. He's in the audience, and you know why I call him my witch doctor? Because whenever I go see him, he tells me which doctor to go to.'

"For the next three weeks on my rounds of the various hospitals in the community, I was the witch doctor! This is a demonstration of Dan's gaiety and wit. But the second side of Dan is different from that. On a cold Thanksgiving morning, I got a call from Dan May. He said, 'I want you to make a housecall.'

"Well, when Dan May says you've got to go, you've got to go. So he came over shortly and I got into his car, and said, 'Dan, where are we going?' And he said, 'To the state penitentiary.' It so happened that Dan had a production manager at the May Hosiery Mills who could really turn out the socks, but he was also imbued with the spirit of ambition and he thought he could do it on his own. So after a while, he left the May Hosiery Mills, went to a little town called Watertown, Tennessee, and built a mill and manufactured socks.

"But they had a fire, the mill burned down, and he collected the fire insurance. But the insurance company that paid off was suspicious, so in due course, the man was tried for arson and sent to the penitentiary. Dan May received a letter from his mother saying the man was sick, and in the ward of the penitentiary medical service, and could he do something for him.

"And, you know, Dan had a great deal of influence in the community. At the state institutions, doors opened wide for him. We went over there and saw this man, and I made a note in the record, and in the next few days the patient was transferred to the

Nashville General Hospital, and treated properly. That was Dan too – a complete lack of vindictiveness and his compassion for mankind."

- Dr. Sam Riven, May's physician

here's only one cure for baldness: You have to shoot your grandfather before you're born.

Surprised.

… responding to inquiries while he was in his late 70s as to how he felt when he woke up in the morning.

The first thing I do when I wake up in the morning is look at the obits and see if I made it through the night. If I'm not listed, I put on my clothes and go to work.

The only good thing about growing old is getting over sex and ambition.

I am going to title my first book *The Joys of Old Age,* and it will consist of nothing but empty pages.

You can tell when you're getting old because you're either trying to remember someone's name or looking for a place to pee.

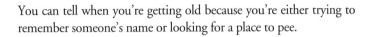

One of the most satisfying results of living a long time is the opportunity to see if people turned out as one would have expected.

The guy who called old age the "golden years" wasn't an assayer by trade.

Three things happen to you when you get old. One, you start forgetting things. The other two I forget.

I am, and I admit it, a terrible hypochondriac. But I have to tell the story of what the hypochondriac had on his tombstone: "I told you I was sick."

I have to remind my doctor that hypochondriacs die too.

I'm sick and tired of waking up sick and tired every morning.

Do you have 30 minutes?

... in his later years, responding to the simple question, "How do you feel?"

A man who hasn't learned how to be his own doctor by the time he is in his forties is not going to live much longer.

If I had known I was going to live this long, I would have taken better care of myself.

The only way to get 30 minute's uninterrupted rest in a hospital is to ring for a nurse.

Hospitals are a very dangerous place to be, especially if you happen to be sick.

I'll never go to a psychiatrist. I think of the centipede who had no problem working all 100 legs until someone asked him how he did it. He stopped to think about it, and never walked again.

The best antidote for suicidal tendencies, say the psychiatrists, is to eat a big meal. It is almost unknown for a man to commit suicide on a full stomach, which demonstrates how transitory these impulses are.

Definition of a gynecologist: A spreader of old wives' tails.

They told me that when I got old that I would lose my mind, but they didn't tell me I wouldn't miss it.

When people ask me how I feel, I have a standard reply: I feel as good as I did forty years ago for about ten minutes every day.

What makes old age unbearable is the loss of one's friends. I remember my father saying when he was 84 that there were only two people left in Nashville who still called him by his first name.

I just went to see my doctor. He told me he found early symptoms of immortality.

When one learns that an acquaintance has passed away, the reflex response often is, "Oh, I didn't know he was dead." Whenever I hear this line, I reply, "I sure hope he's dead because otherwise they've done him a dirty trick. They buried him last week."

I always wondered what colleges without medical schools did with their money.

> ... commenting on the large budget at Vanderbilt Medical School.

For a man with all my symptons, I'm doing pretty well.

I just went in to see my doctor for a physical examination. Afterwards the doctor said, "I don't see anything wrong with you. Why did you come to see me?"

I replied, "I don't feel good."

"How old are you?"

"Seventy-five."

"Get the hell out of here!" responded the doctor. "You're never going to feel good."

I get my exercise as a pallbearer for my friends who were exercise enthusiasts.

I have only missed two days in my office on account of sickness in 40 years! That's what comes from living a pure life and picking good grandparents. My line is, "Have good genes and take care of them."

If aspirin were invented today, the F.D.A. wouldn't approve it.

The life insurance companies have an interesting approach to suicide. Until the Depression, there was only a one-year exclusion on suicide. In other words, a man could take a policy one day and commit suicide a year and a day later, and his family would collect.

Insurance companies knew that if a person would postpone the act for only one year, he wouldn't do it. Most companies have now made it two years, but, according to authorities I read, six months would be adequate. This means that a person (other than a psychotic) would never commit suicide if he would just say to himself, "If the situation hasn't improved in six months, then I will do it."

Suicide is a manifestation of immaturity.

I'm so old, when I was young, I was a little girl.

~3~

Life & Living

**A Man Who Grabs His Hat When the
Speaker Says, "And In Conclusion..."**

"Dan May believed that you could screw up government if you took yourself too seriously. He asked me to make a speech to the Nashville Rotary Club, and he introduced me. He was trying to get Rotarians to look seriously at civic responsibility. I had just returned to Nashville from a stint in the Kennedy administration; that in and of itself made me suspect with most Rotarians.

"But he was certain that if I addressed the club and spoke to the question of commitment in public life, two things would result. One, the Rotarians would get to know me, and this would be beneficial to me and be in the interests of the paper. And two, my own passion for good government was very close to his, and he felt the apparent logic of his position and mine would have an impact on the audience. It would not be just another Monday at Rotary.

"He sat me down beforehand and said, 'John, this is where the community's thinking is, and here's where it needs to be.' He wanted to involve the club in bringing about domestic change in government. But in introducing me, he faced the problem of ensuring that the Rotarians didn't identify him with me. He was afraid they'd think, 'Well, it's just Dan at it again...' He wanted to be certain that in the eyes of the Rotarians, the platform was where I stood, not where we stood together.

"To this day, I've never forgotten how he introduced me. First he gave a brief biography — born, raised, education, entered journalism, known city as a native. He continued, 'The only time Seigenthaler was away from Nashville was in the Kennedy administration, when he was gone for 15 months. During that time, he helped integrate the Deep South. Some damn fool hit him on the head with an iron pipe, and some say he's never been the same since...' That drew a huge laugh.

"Dan went on, 'From the State Capitol, you can see the statue of Edward Ward Carmack, the former editor of **The Tennessean** *who was assassinated because of what he wrote in the newspaper. Many people thought Carmack got what was his due, and that*

the present editor deserves the same fate.' He had them roaring with laughter by then.

"All the while, Dan had that slight but noticeable speech impediment, that gave the whole speech an element of the theater of the absurd. He said very serious things, but the way he rolled his r's and l's really commanded your attention.

"He had nailed me with two very funny hits, but went on to say, 'Whatever your personal or political views, Seigenthaler has something in common with every Rotarian in this room. He shares a deep love of this city, and a deep understanding of how it should work. I present to you, the people of Nashville, someone who loves this city as you do.'

"From that day on, I was accepted by the establishment of Nashville. That's what Dan May could do."

- John Seigenthaler, retired editor and publisher of *The Tennessean*

"Definition of an optimist: A man who grabs his hat when the speaker says, "And in conclusion ..."

Definition of a pessimist: A man in business with an optimist.

Then there was the story about the fellow who went into a restaurant and ordered a turkey sandwich, only to be told by the waitress that they were out of turkey.

"In that case," the fellow said, "let me have a chicken sandwich."

"If we'd had any chicken, you'd have gotten the turkey sandwich," she replied.

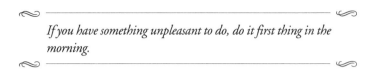

If you have something unpleasant to do, do it first thing in the morning.

Never make any important decisions after midnight.

The average American has two foremost problems: How to keep his weight down, and where to park his car.

I've known many men who have what I call "rare ability." And "rare" is the right word, since one meaning of "rare" is not well-done.

All capable men have a sense of inadequacy.

Don't be afraid to be different. And even more important, don't be afraid to be the same.

Last week I was rummaging through the back of my closet, and I found a crumpled receipt for a watch I had dropped off for repair 12 years ago. I went down to the shop, and there was the same clerk behind the counter. I presented the receipt. The fellow read it, checked his records, and said, "I'll have it ready in three hours. Can you come back?"

I got my work ethic from my father. Pop's cure for all ills was work. When we had pre-school ills, Pop would say, "Go to school. There's nothing wrong with you. Go!"

When we boys were older, the command was the same, except it was, "Go to work!"

Once I told him an acquaintance of his was ill. He quickly replied, "He ain't sick – he's just lazy." A few months went by, and I told Pop he died. He said, "He might as well be dead – he was sick all the time!"

If I had another life to live, I'd come back as twins so that one of us would always be upstairs in bed. With my luck, I'd be the other one.

Better than next year!

… responding to the inquiry, "How's business?"

When I finish this letter and one more, that'll give me two.

The best way to help society is to get a good education, keep informed, and do the best job you can in whatever you do.

There are very few things in life worth worrying about, and most everybody is worrying about the wrong ones.

Three things needed for success: Freedom, ability and a little bit of luck.

Tomorrow you'll be able to say you did this today.

... referring to any mundane event.

"Everthing has been written which could by possibility persuade us that death is not an evil and the weakest men as well as heroes have given a thousand celebrated examples to support this opinion. Nevertheless, I doubt whether any man of good sense ever believed it."

... quoting the 17th century French writer Francois de la Rouchefoucauld in a condolence note.

Do whatever you do...but do it with humor!

There is nothing like possessing a rare and wonderful sense of humor; no man could be my friend who lacked this greatest of all God's minor blessings.

A first-class man will usually get ahead. Remember there is never a good year for a bum show, as they say on Broadway.

In order for the world to be a better place, we don't need x, y or z. We need to remove the shackles from the mind of man.

I live with impending disaster.

Many of our problems stem from this type of thinking, namely that we must be heroic, and that the making of beautiful gestures is more important than accomplishing results.

"Consolation, pressed upon us, when we are suffering under affliction, only serves to increase our pain and to render grief more poignant."

... quoting the Swiss-born French philosopher and 18th century political theorist, Jean Jacques Rousseau.

～4～

Personalities

Between 'Grits' and 'Gesundheit' in the Dictionary

"I used to go camping up in the Ozarks for weeks on end. There are a lot of wild goats up there, and I decided a goat was the most independent, self-reliant beast I ever saw. And Dan May was the greatest old goat I ever knew.

"So when I call someone an old goat, it really has five meanings. One, he's old. Two, he's wise. Three, he's intelligent. Four, an old goat is a man whose thinking is strictly independent and non-conformist. He makes up his own mind. Any old goat does. And most important, having made up his mind, he expresses his opinion to one and all without fear of favor or anything else. That was Dan May."

- Cecil Wray, Nashville businessman and an old friend of May's

"The only place you'll find gratitude is in the dictionary between grits and *gesundheit*.

Then there was the one about the men who had gone on a camping trip. One fellow was sent down to the lake with a bucket to get some drinking water. He came back a few minutes later scared to death.

"You wouldn't believe it," he finally muttered. "There was a big alligator down there."

"Oh for goodness sake," one of his buddies replied. "That alligator is as scared of you as you are of him."

"In that case this water ain't fit to drink!" he said.

Then there was the story about the tightest man in Nashville. One day his horse swallowed a penny, and the man rode the horse backward for a week.

There is no man who became a scoundrel for $1,000 who would not have preferred to be an honest man for half the money.

Whenever I'm in New York City, I walk past a certain apple vendor, and throw him a quarter. But I never take an apple.

Then one day the apple vendor stopped me. I told him I knew what he wanted. I said I bet he wanted to know why I always throw him a quarter and never take an apple.

But the apple vendor said, "No, not at all. I wanted to tell you that the apples have been increased to 35 cents."

Truly classy people always do the right thing automatically. I have to think about it.

I never had the virtue of timidity, if it is a virtue.

If you don't stop telling lies about me, I'm going to start telling the truth about you.

Moderation in all things, including moderation.

Dishonest modesty is not quite as great a sin as blatant egotism, and I try to avoid both.

The fellow has a negative personality. When he enters the room, you have the feeling someone just left.

Being a member of a minority, whether that group is Jewish, black or wealthy, does not excuse one of gross rudeness.

I've never met a man who was 5'11 1/2".

Only the most unusual man ever blames himself for his failure to be as rich or powerful as his neighbor. Mark Anthony's line that "The fault, dear Brutus, is not in the stars, but in ourselves, that we are underlings," is never believed.

Don't ever apologize for diagreeing with me! As long as you have an idea in your head, argue with me. That doesn't mean I will agree with you, but it keeps me on my toes.

Whenever I walk past this beggar in downtown Nashville, I throw him a coin. Then one day I didn't give him anything. The beggar complained.

I said that I was very sorry, but I'd had a bad day at the office.

"Just because you had a bad day, does that mean I have to suffer?" the beggar replied.

I would mention Kipling's short story, "Thrown Away." It is the story of a boy who commits suicide rather than face "disgrace." I put the word disgrace in quotes because what looks like disgrace in one's twenties is held with much tolerance by others. The judgment of an octogenerian as to what constitutes disgrace is tempered greatly by experience.

Disgrace: The definition changes each decade.

Young people often fail to realize how tolerant society is. Your enemies will not excuse you, but who cares?

Let me tell you my idea of a dirty limerick:
   "There once was a girl from Madras,
   Who had a beautiful ass,
   It was not round and pink,
   As you might very well think,
   But was grey, had long ears and ate grass!"

There is a type of men who are mature and have a good sense of values. If they have a fault, I believe it would be the tendency (found in many good men) to indulge the people they love. It is a natural thing to do, but it generally doesn't do the recipient much good, as "things" aren't very important.

The only place to find sympathy is in the dictionary between shit and shovel.

I've always been amused by people who take themselves too seriously. There's the story of the great businessmen who would sit around the club, discussing the great men they had known. Later, one of these great men was relating this conversation to his wife. "You know," he told her, "there aren't many of us great ones left."

"Yes, I know," she replied. "And there's one fewer than you think."

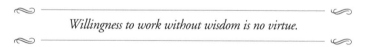

Willingness to work without wisdom is no virtue.

∼ 5 ∼

Religion

Hazy, Lazy and Crazy

"Dan May was a staunch Republican, even though he didn't wear any man's collar; he was his own kind of Republican. He used to complain that I didn't understand anything about economics, and he was quite right. I didn't understand anything about economics, certainly not in any complicated way. I was a New Deal liberal, and I guess I took whatever came down the pike as whatever needed to be done. Dan, who had a much more analytical approach, often would deride my views.

"He felt all rabbis were liberals who didn't understand economics at all. I had to bear the burden of his wrath when the Central Conference of American Rabbis made some statement on social or economic issues. He told me how dumb the rabbis were, and he may have been right. I'm not sure. He didn't realize that our agenda and his were not quite the same. His agenda was more rooted in economic realities; our agenda was rooted in certain kinds of social values. Dan May always forgave me for my ignorance."

- Lou Silberman, former rabbi of The Temple,
Nashville's reform synagogue

"There are three kinds of Jews: hazy, lazy and crazy.

… explaining the three denominations of American Judaism.

When vandals painted swastikas on the Jewish Community Center in Nashville, the local Jewish community was alarmed. I threatened to go over to the Christian Science Church and paint a big "Rx" on the side.

A simple fact of party behavior: Jews say goodbye without leaving. Christians leave without saying goodbye.

Roses are reddish,
Violets are bluish,
If it weren't for Jesus,
You'd all be Jewish!
... opening a speech at the Nashville Rotary club on the topic of Christmas.

Then there was the one about the Jewish fellow who had married a gentile girl. Some years later, the fellow barged into the rabbi's office clutching a newspaper with a banner headline on the front page: HITLER SAYS JEWS IN WORLD-WIDE CONSPIRACY!

"Look here, Rabbi," the fellow said. "I know I married a Catholic, but that's no damn reason not to let me in on this conspiracy!"

I was made a member of the board at The Temple in Nashville, and was often disappointed that much of the discussion at board meetings was not about religious affairs, but about finances. At one meeting, the agenda item under review was how to observe the day of *yahrzeit,* which in the Jewish religion marks the anniversary of the death of a close relative.

A lengthy discussion ensued about how much to charge members of the congregation for the traditional memorial light to remember the deceased. I listened for a while. Finally, I joked, "Why don't we charge $25 for a 25-watt lightbulb, $50 for a 50-watt lightbulb, and for $100 we could have little neon snakes running around the name?"

I was never invited to another meeting.

A dictator-ridden country will eventually become anti-Semitic.

My brother is a pillar of the church. I'm a flying buttress; I support it from without.
    ... May was a non-religious Jew. His brother was an observant Jew.

He's the leading Jewish metallurgist in town.
    ... referring to a local Jewish scrap metal dealer.

That's the great thing about being Jewish: We don't have to worry about doing our Christian duty.

Let me describe for you the difference between a gentile and a Jew. If a gentile puts a coin in a vending machine and it doesn't work, he will curse and kick. If the Jew drops the coin in and it doesn't work, he'll say, "Anti-Semitism."

Reform Jews regard Jesus as a man who lived like a God, whereas Christians regard Jesus as a God who lived like a man.

Jesus Christ was a Jew but not a Christian.

If, when the sun goes down, a Jew in Nashville doesn't have a least two meetings to go to, he is shirking his civic responsibilities.

I had more ham in me than the rabbi approved of.

I'm often asked why the Nashville Jewish community has experienced so little growth over the years. That's easy – every time a Jewish girl gets pregnant, a man leaves town.

The only fairy tales I read are the ones by Hans Jewish Anderson.

Soon after a new rabbi moved to Nashville, I went to The Temple for services on Friday night. The rabbi delivered a sermon that had a strong smattering of left-wing politics in it. Now, I'm a great admirer of reform Judaism, but have often been troubled by the politics of its rabbis.

Shortly thereafter, Dorothy and I invited the rabbi and his wife over for dinner, as was customary. The rabbi was waxing poetic after the meal: "I've been here such a short time and we have already made so many dear friends. One always wonders who one's first enemy will be."

I cut him off. "Quit worrying about the first. You'd better start worrying about the second."

More people have died fighting in the name of religion than for all other ideals.

Tell me, Rabbi, can a Jew save money in a piggy bank?

... cutting in on a bewildered rabbi who was holding forth on the virtues of socialism.

Every law that helps destroy free enterprise is a step toward anti-Semitism. To the economic novice, it may be an amazing concept that German Nazism was both anti-capitalist and anti-Semitic; but to the politically wise, it is an inevitable progression. For it is only by the destruction of free enterprise and the subsequent destruction of democracy that anti-Semitism can take root and thrive.

I'm for the religion of Jesus – but not so much for the religion about Jesus.

One of my favorite stories involves my old friend Harvie Branscomb, the former chancellor of Vanderbilt and an ordained Methodist minister. Both he and I were born on Christmas day.

I always told Chancellor Branscomb that I had one big advantage on him. Every year on Good Friday I'm scared to death. Any Jewish boy who's born on Christmas, if he gets by Good Friday, he knows he's good for another year. It doesn't apply to Methodists!

I am catholic in my religion.

I would be less than truthful if I did not indicate that there might be some negative factors if the United States adopted a culture of poverty. The most serious one, as I see it, would be that our rabbis would be at a total loss for subjects for sermons on Rosh Hashonah eve. For more years than I care to recall, I have heard them berate businessmen and conservatives. Once we had poverty with socialism, I am afraid they might have to dig up a new subject, *mirabile dictu.*

My brother is such an ardent Zionist that whenever he fills out his passport application, he fills in "Jew" under profession.

~6~

Business & Commerce

Give, Get or Git

"We were at a commencement at Vanderbilt, and it was dull. I was sitting next to Dan, and that was the only thing that kept me sane. This was back before facial hair had become well-accepted, and some professor came by with a scraggly beard. Dan leaned over and whispered to me, 'I can never understand why anyone would cultivate on his face what grows wild on his ass.'

"When Dan was a student at Vandy, he was the most liberal fellow in the world. By the time he died, he was the most conservative. But I never knew Dan to be on the wrong side of things. He never gave cause for anyone to doubt where he stood.

"Dan did not like pomposity, sham or conceit. He had no time for stuffiness. You always knew where he stood. He always said to me, 'Andy, you're the only banker I know with a sense of humor; there's none of that in your business.' And if Dan said, it, you believed him."

- Andrew Benedict, former chairman of the First American Bank of Nashville, and a fellow member of the Vanderbilt University Board of Trust

"Three "G's" of charitable board membership: Give, get, or git.

Definition of business ethics: In business, a man will do almost anything to make money. That "almost" is business ethics.

During the depression we had a customer who bought 100 dozen socks from us. He bought them in January. February, March, April and May went by and he still hadn't paid for them. In June, I got a telegram from him to send another 100 dozen socks.

I sent him a polite letter and said, "We can't ship your new order until you pay for the last shipment."

He wired back, "Cancel the new order; I can't wait that long."

The fire at that manufacturing plant was due to friction caused by a large inventory rubbing up against an insurance policy.

Definition of an actuary: A man without enough personality to be an accountant.

Then there was the story about the fellow who bought a pig for $200 in the fall, and fattened him up all winter on $200 worth of feed. Then he sold the pig in the spring for $400. He didn't make any money, but he did have use of the pig!

A fellow walked into a country store one day where a huge inventory of salt was displayed on the floor. He commented on the barrels of salt to the owner. "That's nothing," the owner replied. "Let me take you downstairs."

They went downstairs, and the entire basement was filled with salt. "You must sell a lot of salt," the fellow said.

"No, not really," the owner replied. "But the guy who sells the salt to me does."

Never hire a man who smokes a pipe. You'll never get more than half a day's work out of him.

There were two brothers in Georgia who bought watermelons for $1.00 in the country, then drove to the city where they sold them for $12.00/dozen.

One brother noticed, "We're not making any money this way."

"All we need is a bigger truck," said the other.

The secret of any business is to buy by the carload and sell by the ounce.

One day a man from the phone company came out to the May Hosiery Mills after I inquired about getting a long extension cord for my phone. I asked what it would cost.

"Eighty-nine cents a month," the man said.

"In that case, I don't need it," I replied.

"What? What's 89 cents a month to a big company like the May Hosiery Mills?" the man asked.

"I guess you're right," I told him. "Let's just forget the charge. What's 89 cents a month to a big company like the phone company?"

Three "W's" of board membership: Wealth, wisdom and work.

A banker will lend you an umbrella on a clear day, but when it starts to rain, he'll take it back.

You don't have to be real bright to be a banker. All you need to know is that 4% is less than 5%.

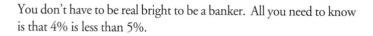

Then there's the one about the fellow whose parents are in the iron and steel business. His mother irons and his father steals.

During the depression, one of Nashville's fine society ladies came out to the May Hosiery Mills and wanted some socks for her charity. The mill was losing money hand over fist.

She said, "I need 60 dozen pairs of socks, and be sure to let me have them at cost."

"You're a fool," I told her. "You'd better take the selling price. I wish to heck I could get cost!"

Never borrow money except for a primary residence, education, or emergency health problems.

I learned a long time ago how to make the summer months pass quickly. Borrow money in June, make the note payable in three months, and fall will be here before you know it.

Stay out of banks. You may never get as rich as you could with other people's money and some luck, but the trade-off is sleeping at night. Live your life so you can walk down Fourth Avenue with mistletoe on your coattail.

I have always avoided contact with the stereotypical banker. I despise the professional type. He caters to the rich and powerful, hovers over them, laughs at their heavy-handed feeble attempts at humor, flatters them and embraces them with a total disregard for how they obtained their wealth.

Miss Jones, the ribbon clerk at F. W. Woolworth, has resigned her position to devote herself fulltime to her hair.

The best bankers have a job to do for their employers but they do not bootlick. They get business for their banks without being sychophantic, hypocritical prostitutes.

One day I walked into the Third National Bank in Nashville and struck up a conversation with my banker. "How's money?" I asked.

"Oh, it's tough," the banker replied. "Things are tight."

"Good," I said. "I've got a little cash, and I'd like to buy a certificate of deposit."

"Look here, you son-of-a-gun," said the surprised banker. "The next time you walk into this bank, tell me if you're buying or selling!"

If you have to ask what it costs, you can't afford it.

I'd be happy to carry that ad on my license plate if you pay me $200. Otherwise, take it off.
        ... directed at Nashville auto dealers who sold new cars with the name of their dealership displayed prominently on the border of the license plate.

I had a memorable conversation one day with a Jewish friend in Nashville who was just back from a trip to Montreal, where she had bought a fur coat.

"The coat was so cheap it paid for the trip," she said.

"Why didn't you buy two coats," I asked, "and take your husband along?"

The Vanderbilt Board of Trust doesn't need any more millionaires. What we need now is multi-millionaires!

My idea of a genius is a man who can buy something from Will Weaver and sell it to Ralph Ewing and make a profit.

... on two Tennessee businessmen.

If I had to start my career over again, I'd find something that cost a nickel to make, sold for a dollar, and was habit-forming.

Nobody can advise you on insurance; they're either trying to sell it to you or they don't understand it.

Excuse me, but could you tell me if you are standing up or sitting down?

...a standard telephone line for obnoxious salesmen. If his caller were sitting, May would say, "Why don't you stand up and shove that phone up your ass?" And if he were standing, "Good. Why don't you shove...."

I'm awful glad I'm in the Rotary Club. I'll never have to buy insurance from a stranger.

People shop for what they pay, not what they buy.

The stock market is a lot like a horse race, except in a horse race only one horse can win.

I have known many men who knew when to buy, but it takes a genius to know when to sell. People always want to sell when they are in trouble. The only time to sell a business is when it is prosperous.

7

Politics

Once He's Bought, He Stays Bought

"**D**efinition of an honest politician: Once he's bought, he stays bought.

After I lost a race for the Nashville Metro Council, a reporter asked about my supposed exit from public life. I told the reporter that I was reminded of the man who owned an entry in the Kentucky Derby.

This man thought he'd give his horse some extra incentive, so he mixed a half-gallon of moonshine whiskey with the animal's pre-race breakfast oats. The reporter asked if the horse won the race.

No, he didn't, I told him. But he was one of the happiest losers you ever saw in your life.

Tennessee's State Legislature: The best that money can buy.

I would love to hear some politician show the same concern about the person from whom he takes the dollar as he does about the individual to whom he is giving it.

God plus one is a majority.

The argument is made that if a man is old enough to fight for his country, he should be old enough to vote. By the same logic, a man who is too old to fight for his country should be prohibited from voting.

It has now become the duty of government to take care of all special groups but without saying at whose expense. Shouldn't some thought be given to the man who takes care of his own possible misfortune?

If I ever go back to Vanderbilt, I'm going to write my Ph.D. thesis on who has done more harm to America – the out-and-out scoundrels or the well-intentioned damn fools.

> *... May applied the term "well-intentioned damn fools" to those he considered impractical Democrats, or limousine liberals.*

Too many of America's liberals are under the mistaken impression that they have a monopoly on morality.

I was a Republican down South when it was considered an underground movement.

Viscount Montgomery classified his generals into three groups: (1) smart and active; (2) stupid and lazy; and (3) stupid and active. The first group won the war for him. The second could always be placed in charge of a depot or somewhere where they could do no harm.

It was the third group that drove him mad. Similarly, in politics. I believe the crooked politician isn't nearly as troublesome as the stupid ones who think they are leading a crusade for something good when they are actually 100% wrong.

Definition of an honest politician: One who honestly didn't know what his supporters had done to get him elected.

I am firmly convinced that the solution to all problems – political, economic, social, medical or any other adjective ending in "al" – will never be found with an ignorant electorate.

Except for being President, being mayor of a big city is the most impossible job. You won't do a good job, because no one can. Within a short time, one or both of our local papers will ridicule and revile you and your coronary artieries will react.

A true liberal must be constantly on guard to see that the individual never loses any of his rights in return for a false security.

A liberal is someone who is farther away from the situation than you are. I've always been troubled by the white "liberals" of Nashville who were strong advocates of busing when it was a Mississippi issue but were quick to enroll their kids in private schools when integration came to Tennessee.

I try to be liberal without being foolish, and conservative without being reactionary.

Scratch any successful American and you will find beneath the skin a frustrated politician. We are all a nation of political Walter Mittys, and the most universal dream of glory is a political one.

Had the Republicans controlled the House and Senate during Nixon's term of office, Watergate never would have been heard of. I know this does not justify what was done but, as a practical politician, I have always recognized that the greatest vice is not having the adequate number of votes.

The radicals of one generation are the conservatives of the next. So often the conservatives can be defined as individuals who revere dead radicals.

Dear Mr. Paxton:

One of your publicity men, an actor named Ronald Reagin (I hope I have spelled his name correctly), spoke before the local Rotary Club about a month ago. He makes a very popular type of a speech and much that he said contained truth. On the other hand, much that he said was utter rot. He is a clever speaker and received a standing ovation, although I noticed that the more intelligent men in the group either kept their seats or rose reluctantly.

The worst thing he does is to cast aspersions on higher education and, athough said in semi-humor, he intimated that Harvard deserved to be considered an object of ridicule.

I have a lot of interests, among which education and economics are not the least. To hear a General Electic man intimate that Hollywood is more important than Harvard, and to hear him further demonstrate that his knowledge of economics is rather perfunctory adds little to the prestige of the company.

The case for American business should be presented by intelligent men. This is not the same thing as saying it must be presented in a dull manner.

Yours very truly...

... in a letter penned May 26, 1959, to Robert Paxton, president of General Electric Co.

Why are college professors overwhelmingly Democrats? A college professor is searching for the truth. Truth is elusive, and can only be found by experimental trial and error. The college professor is accustomed to research and to experiments that usually end in failure, but he still persists in searching for the truth, or he would be denying the first axiom of pure scholarship. Researchers cannot be interested in the immediate day-to-day problems, but must concentrate on the long-range search for truth. The absent-minded professor, in searching for the truth, runs the risk of stepping in an open manhole, but that does not deter him.

~8~

Leisure

Obesity Doesn't Run in Families

"Obesity doesn't run in families; good cooks do.

That restaurant was so dark that I didn't know what I ate until I went home and burped.

What did Jesus say at the last supper? Anyone who wants to get in the picture come over to my side of the table!

No matter where they put the coach's box, the thirdbase coach will stand somewhere else.

I told my friend Wendell Phillips that if he died, I'd be the sloppiest man in Nashville. And, by God, he died.

There's a failsafe solution for what to do if you get lost in the forest. You get some gin, some vermouth and an olive, and mix them in a glass. Some fellow is sure to come along and say, "That's not the way to make a martini. Let me show you!" Then ask that fellow how to get out of the forest.

I buy my clothing from Joe Frank, but he insists on one thing — that I put R.Z. Levy's label in the coat, because he doesn't want to get the blame for the way I look.

... about two Nashville clothing merchants.

That's the best dinner I've ever eaten.
... to his wife, every night.

My wife is a most resourceful lady. She bought a subscription to the *El Paso Times,* and every time it rains in El Paso, she waters her cactus.

During World War II, when labor was scarce, I cut our grass twice. That's the first and last time I ever did it.

I took my wife to a fancy restaurant once, but she embarrassed me by dropping her tray.

I just came back from a party. Everyone asked after you. The pigs asked, the cows asked, the horse's ass too!

Advice to a child before going out on a date: Don't do anything tonight that you wouldn't do in Macy's window.

Prostitution was once a thriving business in Nashville, but it has almost disappeared thanks to the automobile and the amateurs.

How about right after this drink?
   ... responding to a surprised waitress who was refilling his glass and said, "Say when."

Formula for avoiding friends' boring vacation stories and photographs: When they get back, stay away from them twice as many days as they've been gone.

Then there was the time Goldstein was in the restaurant and came back from the bathroom. He started complaining to the guy who owned the restaurant, "I washed my hands but when I went to dry them all I could find was this nasty old washrag."

"You know, Goldstein," the proprietor responded, "I've been in business for years, and thousands of customers have used that washrag. Why all of a sudden are you complaining?"

I never eat jello. I don't like eating anything more nervous than I.

Advice on packing: Take twice as much money and half as many clothes as you think you'll need.

I have no sympathy for anyone with an ice cream headache.

Two reasons to wear clothes: Vanity and modesty.

For years the May Hosiery Mills made a popular line of cumbersome, long cotton hosiery for women. I used to jest, "You know what happens to women who wear our long cotton hosiery? Nothing!"

No, thank you. It might keep me awake during the program.
        ... refusing coffee with his meal, just before the luncheon speeches began.

I divide my friends into two groups: Those who understand the comic strip *Peanuts*, and those who think it's crazy and meaningless. I don't associate with the latter group much.

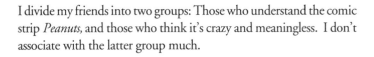

The miniskirts aren't going to get any shorter. The end is in sight.

There has never been a man more disinterested in food than I. I am not an epicure, a gourmet or a gourmand, although I have never known the difference among these words.

Father's Day is a horrible commercialization of a wholesome sentiment.

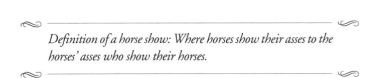

Definition of a horse show: Where horses show their asses to the horses' asses who show their horses.

You know my methods; apply them.
... Sherlock Holmes, explaining to his sidekick Dr. Watson how to solve a mystery.
These are the same words May said to his children when they
left for any new venture such as freshman year at college.

Whenever I arrive in a new city, I always give the same instructions to the taxi driver in order to get my bearings: "Show me where the richest man in town lives, and where the poorest man in town lives."

Then there was the story attributed to a flamboyant magistrate in Nashville in the early twentieth century. A prostitute appeared in the magistrate's court and wanted a man arrested for giving her gonorrhea.

The magistrate said he didn't believe that this was an indictable offense, then hesitated a moment and said, "We'll arrest him for arson; he set your place of business on fire."

The inscription on the waiter's tombstone: By and by, God caught his eye.

... on slow restaurant service.

I tell everybody the same thing. If you go to bed early for about three weeks and eat lightly, you will feel almost as well as you did before you went on your vacation.

~9~

People

Any Ordinary Guy Away from Home with a Briefcase

"It was clear that Dan was not an organized temple-goer. But if any bigot cast a stone toward Jews or Judaism, Dan was there at the forefront of combatting bigotry at all levels. Somehow he got the methods and teachings of prophetic Judaism through in the life he led. This was much better than being a regular worshiper, and forgetting all that you learned in temple before you got to your car.

"Dan was part of a very small power structure that made up the local Jewish community. We all admired him so much in so many ways: business, educational, political, civic, religious. A man like Dan, because of who he was, just commanded respect.

"When Dan walked around the floor of the mill, those workers were dedicated to him. Whenever there was a family crisis, the word was that Dan was supportive. If Suzy the looper had some problem, then Dan or the May Hosiery Mills would help her out. But you never heard about it from Dan. You'd hear about it from a friend that night, but word got around."

- Jack Kuhn, retired Nashville retail executive, and member of the local Jewish community

"Definition of an expert: Any ordinary guy away from home with a briefcase.

Giving gratuitous advice to others is an egregious error as a rule.

Then there was the story about one of Nashville's outspoken magistrates in the early 20th century. The magistrate had a small paperweight on his desk, a replica of the famous trio of monkeys who were free from evil.

After both defendant and plaintiff in a civil case had their say, one young attorney apparently asked to be allowed to speak for 30 minutes on his client's behalf. The magistrate said that that was all right, but he was going out to get a haircut and, when the young attorney had finished, he could find the court's judgment under the monkeys.

I have little patience for people who put on airs or make false promises.

I love the story about the rookie baseball player at his first big league spring training camp.

On Monday he sent home a postcard, "Hitting the heck out of the ball." Tuesday's postcard read, "Everything's great. I'm a cinch to head north with the team."

Finally, on Wednesday, came the last card, "They started throwing curves. I'll be home Saturday."

Then there was the one about the fellow who used memory devices to remember names. This fellow had a friend named Mrs. Hummock, and remembered that it rhymed with stomach.

Next time he saw her, the fellow promptly said, "Hello, Mrs. Kelly."

It is better to be disliked than unnoticed.

The biggest and toughest job in any position close to the people is to shut up longwinded citizens at public meetings without making them angry.

A sure way to make an enemy is to do someone a favor.

I often hear it said that we should not judge people. We have taste in wine and art; it's ridiculous to think we should not have taste in people.

I was often entertained at the Nashville home of an eccentric friend whose wife was without doubt the worst housekeeper in the civilized world. Dogs, cats, monkeys, parrots were everywhere, and at one dinner a cat (or was it a dog?) jumped on the table during dinner and walked its whole length.

Meals were served at any hour, or totally omitted, and dinner started at any time from 7:00 to 10:30 p.m. At one never-to-be-forgotten dinner, the butler came to the living room door at 9 p.m. and announced in solemn tones, "Gentleman, dinner is not served."

The executive son-in-law.
… moniker for any fellow who married into the family business.

I lobbied for years to get a black member on the Vanderbilt Board of Trust. Finally, Bishop Joseph Johnson became in 1971 the first black to join the board by regular election. When Bishop Johnson, a clergyman and educator of some note, came to his first meeting, he was formally inducted, and welcomed to the board. It was hoped that Bishop Johnson would provide some insights on minority issues at Vanderbilt, which were then a highly controversial topic. (This he did admirably).

Bishop Johnson sat through most of the first meeting without saying a word. Finally, an issue came up that aroused his attention, and he decided to speak. "Mr. Chairman," he began, "My wife told me not to open my mouth, and if I opened it, to be brief." Bishop Johnson then launched into a powerful 20-minute exposition– using the full powers of ministry training – and even included several arcane scriptural references.

When he finally finished, the rest of the board was silent. I spoke first. "Bishop," I joked, "you should have listened to your wife."

For years, whenever there was a meeting of the Jewish Community Center in Nashville, I would receive a phone call from Sabena Grief, the secretary at the Center. She was a woman of habit, and would always start her conversation the same way: "This is Sabena." Then she would predictably proceed with the details of the upcoming meeting.

After I retired, my wife and I were touring Europe and found ourselves in an out-of-the-way hotel in Athens, Greece. The phone rang, and I answered it. A female voice promptly said, "This is Sabena."

I was stunned. "How did you find me here?" I finally stammered.

It was, of course, an agent from the national carrier of Belgium, Sabena Airlines, confirming the return flight.

❧ 10 ❧

Places

Winter and Next Winter

"Dan May was the first liberal Republican I ever knew. He first persuaded me that you could both be liberal and Republican. When I first knew Dan, I was just a little fellow. Before I ever took office, Dan called upon me to help the old city board of education many times. Having children in the school system, I was sympathetic.

"Then I ran for county judge. We had many of the tremendous problems of dividing the county dollar between school systems. And Dan and I were thrown together. He invited me for lunch, and I always knew that he was going to buy me a cheap lunch and it was going to cost the county a fortune.

"During those lunches, Dan would tell me how to run Davidson County. He did it so well I knew I had an expert. And I decided I could run it better if I changed the membership of the Davidson County Court. I told Dan the only way I could run the county right was to get some good men in the county court. The city of Nashville at that time had some 19 members of the court, and I got to thinking that Dan May's name should be number one on the list.

"He looked at me and kind of grinned, and said his business was working at the mill making hosiery. He kind of rubbed me off a little bit, but I pushed it along during the lunch. About three weeks later, he called me on the phone and said, 'Were you serious?' I said I'd never uttered anything but a serious word in my life, and that was one of the most serious. Needless to say, we won that election, and Dan May came to the county court.

"Dan May was always the one on the firing line and I think he and I made a lot of people mad at us at times. We both pushed so hard. For thirty-some years, from the time I was a young lawyer, I saw the insights that Dan May had and the involvement that he took upon himself as a businessmen in the community. He was not just a businssman, he was a man of concern.

"Dan was a man who probably had a little deeper in his heart the teachings of Judaism than a lot of people I knew who attend the temple more regularly than he did. I do not know a man who I have a higher respect for, and a higher regard for, and this community has a greater debt to. I don't know how to speak of Dan May except in superlatives."

- Beverly Briley, former Mayor of Nashville

"There are only two seasons in Alaska: Winter and next winter.

Once there was a little boy in Nashville who came home from school and said, "I helped a policeman today."

"How?" he was asked.

"His horse dropped dead on Demonbreun Street and he didn't know how to spell it."

"So you spelled it for him?"

"No. I helped him drag it to 8th Avenue!"

Then there's the story about the time a circus visited a remote prairie town and an elephant escaped. A few hours later, the police received a phone call from a frantic housewife. "There's a huge bull loose in my garden," she said. "He's picking my cabbages with his tail, and if I told you where he's putting them, you wouldn't believe it."

How about the fellow who bought a sugar cane plantation in Jamaica? The fellow was having problems with rats in the fields. He tried cats, poison and traps, but nothing worked. So he decided to write his friend in the U.K.

In the letter, he explained the rat problem, and asked his friend to "send two mongeese." That didn't look right, so he tore it up and wrote a second letter requesting "two mongooses." Still, it looked funny, so he tried a third draft, asking for "two mongoose."

Finally, he wrote a letter which he was sure got it right: "Dear so and so," he began. "Please send me a mongoose." Then he signed his name and added, "p.s. Send another one!"

The best way to judge a country is by whether people are trying to get into it, or out of it.

I never take any unnecessary risks. During World War II, I thought about painting "Oak Ridge" on the roof of the May Hosiery Mills in Nashville in big bright Japanese letters with an arrow pointing east.

> *… Oak Ridge, the site of America's atomic bomb research laboratory, is located about 175 miles due east of Nashville.*

You know how people got to the other side of this street? They were born over there!

> *… said of a busy intersection.*

Do you know why all the satellite cities around Nashville have "hills" in their names? Because none of them is on the level.

> *… of Forest Hills, Green Hills, etc.*

МЕЖДУНАРОДНЫЙ ГАЗОВЫЙ СОЮЗ

ПОВЕСТКА ДНЯ
очередного заседания МГС в Москве
2-4 августа 1960 г.

1. Приветствие Председателя НТО нефтяной и газовой промышленности СССР СОРОКИНА А.И.

2. Ответное приветствие Президента Международного Газового Союза Б.М.НИЛЬСОНА.

3. Утверждение разосланного Протокола заседания Совета Между - народного газового Союза, состоявшегося в Праге 4-5 апреля 1960 года.

4. Технический прогресс в строительстве магистральных газопроводов в СССР.
   Доклад Начальника Главгаза СССР КОРТУНОВА А.К.

5. Опыт эксплуатации магистральных газопроводов.
   /Сообщения национальных газовых ассоциаций Франции, Италии, Канады, Чехословакии и СССР/.

6. О ходе подготовки к Международному Газовому конгрессу в Стокгольме в 1961 году /Информация генерального секретаря МГС Р.Х.ТУВЕЛДА и всех членов МГС/.

7. Рассмотрение рекомендаций МГС постоянной рабочей группе по газу Европейской Экономической Комиссии ООН в Женеве по унификации правил проектирования и строительства магистральных газопроводов /Информация газовой ассоциации Нидерландов, США и СССР/.

8. Рекомендации национальных газовых ассоциаций Швеции, Румынии, Франции, ФРГ и СССР о создании новых Комитетов МГС.

9. Прием новых газовых организаций в члены МГС.

10. Разное.

Заседания Совета будут происходить в конференц-зале Дома Дружбы с народами зарубежных стран /ул.Калинина, 16/

... after May returned from a short visit to the Soviet Union, he agreed to address the Nashville Rotary Club. He was asked to write a short summary of his speech for advance publicity. His submission, which was distributed verbatim by the club's secretary, is above.

I don't know why anyone would want to live in Belle Meade. You've got the sun in your eyes in the morning going to work, and then, when you come home at night, you get the sun in your eyes again.

... on an affluent suburb five miles west of Nashville's city center.

───────────────────────────────────────

Summer heat: In New York, it's an attack; in Nashville, it's a siege.

───────────────────────────────────────

I live one Wing-Ding cup and two Kentucky Fried Chicken boxes down from Hillsboro.

... on the litter in his neighborhood.

───────────────────────────────────────

After I returned to Nashville from a trip to Italy, I used to ask what kind of people lived in the Po Valley. The answer? " 'Po folk" of course.

───────────────────────────────────────

I love the flag, but you'd think my pledge would be good for more than one week.

... wondering why the pledge was recited every week before the Nasvhille Rotary Club.

Once we have been successful in reducing the lot of the North American to that of the South American, our embassies will be safe from rock-throwing and we, the U.S.A., will become as popular as we should love to be.

... from a popular, facetious speech titled "How to Create Poverty."

X x Y x Z = the Fruition of the Great American Dream.

X = the power and strength of our military arms.

Y = the value we place on the American ideals.

Z = the degree of courage we have to use military force, to use everything in our command to preserve the items in second term Y. All of you know enough algebra to know that X times Y times Z equals Zero if any of the three terms equals zero. We will not survive, no matter how strong our arms may be, if we falter in our dedication to American freedom or if our courage is chicken.

I don't claim to be an authority on the Soviet Union just because I was there for five days. But you don't have to walk far in a sewer to know that it smells bad.

I have often asked brilliant minds why America is such a great country. One standard answer is that we have got great natural resources. No denying that. But important as these are, they are not the sole or most important reason, for Bolivia, Mexico, Venezuela, Saudi Arabia and Siberia have as much or more per square mile, yet they are poor compared with us.

Another routine answer is that we have been spared the ravages of war, which is hardly true. The desolation of a large part of America – Tennessee, Georgia, North and South Carolina, Virginia, and several other states to a lesser extent – in the years 1861-1865 has rarely been equalled. And I don't recall any war of consequence in South America, or India, or Africa.

I also say it wasn't God-given. God didn't think any more of Americans than anyone else.

It comes from a lot of things that we must preserve. Foremost among them is our free society.

~11~

Public Affairs & Daily Events

If I Had My Life to Live Over Again...

"Dan May was open. If he told you something, that was it. You could use it. He was always on the level. He believed that government had to operate in the public view. May was one of the first Jews to be elected to city-wide office in Nashville, and he was known as a liberal also. And he was outspoken. How'd he do it? There's no single answer. It's a tribute to his ability, and the respect so many people had for him.

"He was always accessible. He'd never give you a 'no comment.' May always liked newspaper people. Now, he wouldn't hesitate to tell you if you quoted him out of context. But he was an extrovert, and scrupulously fair and honest.

"May had a great trust in the people. He felt that once they had all the facts, they would make the right decisions. He was probably ahead of his time. But, despite his contributions, he was not awed by the position he held. He had that delightful sense of humor. He was a highly intelligent person, and well-educated, but he could sit on the street corner and talk to anyone.

"He always wanted to know your ideas. When you talked to May, you'd go home and say to your wife, 'That councilman is a damn smart man; he asked me what I thought about such-and-such.' If you talked to Al Gore Sr., he'd give you a 30-minute lecture, and you'd tell your wife, 'What a stupid man!'"

- Wayne Whitt, former managing editor of *The Tennessean*

"I f I had my life to live over again, I'd live over a delicatessen.

Best day of the year, 'cept one.

... punning on the first day of September.

Your emcee thinks I am like a vending machine; all you have to do is drop in a dinner and up comes a speech. But there's one big difference between him and me; all he has to do is drop in a speech and up comes your dinner.

... at a public dinner, when the master of ceremonies wound up the evening by calling on May, without advanced warning, to "say something funny."

It doesn't say, "positively."

... explaining why he had ignored a traffic sign he hadn't cared for.

Why do faucets drip? Because they can't go like this.

... sniffing in hard and feigning a runny nose.

I sent him a nice, diplomatic letter. I spelled "bastard" with a capital B.

Houseguests are like dead fish ... after a few days they start to stink.

As the delicatessen man said, all this and herring too!

... acknowledging any situation of abundance.

I rank drivers. Two people in the front seat are worse than one. Old drivers are worse than young. Country drivers are worse than city, women worse than men.

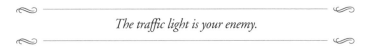

The traffic light is your enemy.

Let some issue come up that involves the public interest, and only preachers, screwballs and the president of the League of Women Voters will show up at the public meeting.

We must make our citizens feel like participants rather than victims.

Attorneys have a disease, possibly malignant, namely they must find something wrong with any instrument sent to them by another attorney.

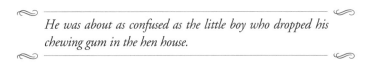

He was about as confused as the little boy who dropped his chewing gum in the hen house.

Whenever I received a foolish letter that was the result of a bureaucratic snafu, I'd write back that the letter had been referred to the Office of Utter Confusion and Hysteria, commonly known as OUCH.

Whenever I was involved in public debate, I'd use the same tactic when I felt my counterpart was twisting my words, or talking nonsense. I'd tell of the young man who said to a young girl at their first meeting, "I am a man of few words; do you or don't you?"
    The young girl replied, "I don't, but I will. You've out-talked me."

If all the cars in Tennessee were lined up from end to end, the driver in the front car would stall her engine.

You could block more traffic if you parked it sideways.
    ... offering unsolicited advice to a man who was double-parked on a busy street.

So often "emergencies" have the habit of becoming chronic. I'm skeptical of "emergency" laws, particularly to raise taxes, since I never saw one that didn't become permanent.

Everything else can await, "everything else" covering the gamut from Alpha to Omaha, as Ring Lardner always said.
    ... concluding a business letter.

In spite of the menace of Russia and in spite of two world wars, I still envy my grandchildren. The progress we made economically, scientifically, yes, even morally, will be accelerated in the next 50 years at a geometric rate. My grandchildren, when they get to their seventh decade, will look upon Montgomery and Little Rock as we regard the witch trials at Salem.

The atomic age is here to stay, but are we?

Fourteen hundred years ago the Roman Empire ended, and Gibbon, in his history of the rise and fall of the Roman Empire, lists the following reasons for its fall:

1. Excessive spending by the government
2. The unwillingness of young men to bear arms and fight for their nation
3. Overindulgence in luxury
4. Breakdown in morality and easy divorce, which weakened family life
5. Excessive effeminacy, with the boys and men dressing and acting like women, and the women like men
6. Breakdown and drifting away from religion

Sad comment: Seems each generation fails to read the minutes of the last one.

We should remember one thing that the greybeards do not tell us: Although history repeats itself, the repetitions are not identical, for if they were, every college sophomore could diagnose the future without error.

Today the telephone has ruined the prospects of 21st-century historians.

It is most difficult to write laws controlling big masses of the population without running the danger that they will be administered unjustly.

I've had my fill of (a) second-class lawyers, and (b) first-class lawyers who know all the law, but who don't win cases.

Our senators will never vote against any well-organized minority. There are more stockholders in the U.S. than there are members of unions, but the former are unorganized.

Nothing was good about the good old days except one thing. I was young then. And that was good.

Advice for public speaking: Never repeat anything for emphasis. I say, never repeat anything for emphasis.

Once I was locked in a legal battle, and sent several letters to the opposing attorneys. They failed to respond. Finally, I penned a short note: "I didn't realize my halitosis extended to my correspondence."

Then there was the Nashville attorney whose wife was known to be a "literary" person. One day, the lawyer was elected a magistrate of the Nashville County Court.

When the fellow came home and told his wife of his new title, she reportedly asked him, "What does that make me?"

He replied, "The same damn fool you've always been!"

The only way to avoid guests is to have a one-bedroom house with no baths.

Company's here. Get out the toothpicks.
… said whenever unexpected guests showed up just before supper

~12~

Social Commentary

Traffic Cop, Homeplate Umpire, and the American Press

*"You would think that summarizing a few highlights of Dan May's activities in and on behalf of the community wouldn't have been much of a job. All I'd have to do, I said to myself, was to go down to **The Banner** library, ask Sally to pull the Dan May file, and spend half an hour taking notes and then call it quits. It wasn't that way.*

"I didn't have any trouble getting Sally to cooperate. The file was there all right, all five or six tightly packed envelopes, dating back 30 years or more. But when I started going back over time, remembering and filling in the gaps from my own contacts and associations with Dan May, when I found all the dates and events recorded, it didn't tell the story of Dan May at all.

"Over the years, my affection for him grew steadily. Because secretly, and sometime openly, I agreed with every damn thing he said. Dan May always was as a public figure, a good newspaper man's prayer. And I think I was a damn good newspaper man at one time.

"In public utterance, he was never coy, shy or the type to hide behind a lot of useless conversation, which serves only to clutter up what otherwise was a good story. He was available, articulate, candid, explicit and — when he wanted to be — quick with the wit and humor that laughed at himself as easily as he laughed at the foibles of others.

"Dan May has brightened, enlivened, sometimes exasperated many solemn sessions with his own brand of wit, humor, and true, plain-spoken common sense. Dan May can't be summed up or described in a resume. Every story, every incident that comes up reminds you of something else. Dan May was incomparable."

- **Dick Battle**, former political columnist, *The Banner*

"There are three people with whom you can never win an argument: A traffic cop, a home plate umpire, and the American press.

... occasionally told with four people, adding your wife.

Two occupational characteristics of newspaper people: Alcoholism and monumental conceit.

The stinkers who control our media all suffer from the Jehovah Complex, namely, they get themselves mixed up with God.

The best thing about *The Banner* is that you can pick it up at the end of your driveway and have it read by the time you get to your trash can at the back.

...on Nashville's afternoon newspaper.

I've often been accused of talking "awful plainly" in public. I respond by telling about the fellow who said, "I'm marrying a beautiful girl. She comes from a fine family. She is extremely rich, she's talented and she has a wonderful background. And on top of that, she has syphilis."
The other fellow said, "Is that good?"
"It must be good. *The Banner* is against it!"

I prefer *The Tennessean* to the evening TV news because at least you can wrap up your garbage in it.

...commenting on Nashville's morning paper.

When one starts a sentence to a black man with the phrase, "in the long run you will be better off if ...," he will rightly answer you that in the long run he will be dead.

I was for black rights when the subject was almost taboo locally. In the track meet of life, I believe everyone should be given as equal a start as possible, but the race shouldn't be a tie for all entries. On the other hand, you shouldn't win by kicking the other fellow to make him lose.

We seldom lose all our liberty at one time. The loss of liberty is an insidious, creeping diease and, offtimes, it is sold to us under the guise of social betterment and security.

There is one thing and one thing only that will create a sudden war at any time, and that is a conviction that we are appeasers.

The history of man has shown that free societies do not last forever. We prefer not to think of the death of anything, especially that of ourselves or our society. But history demonstrates that free societies generally lose zest, and the desire for freedom is at its highest, only when it is un-obtainable, not when it is being enjoyed.

If the Bill of Rights, which is the basis of our American freedom, were introduced in Congress today, I doubt it would get out of the Senate committee.

We must not lose our freedom. We must not lose our liberty. You only experiment with dictators once.

Feminism is the biggest bunch of nonsense since Christianity.

I was asked to address a national convention of school administrators in Atlantic City in 1948. They seemed to want me on the program since I was Southern, active in the civil rights movement and a two-term member of Nashville's old city school board.

As was expected, one of the right-wing delegates soon challenged me for my "liberal" stand on integration. "Would you want your daughter to marry a Negro?" the delegate asked.

"No," I replied. "I wouldn't want my daughter to marry any gentile."

The black will not be on an economic par with whites until his education and social consciousness are equal to that of whites.

The promise and the victory at Appomattox were lost to the black by political devices in the Congress for almost 100 years. The first Civil Rights bill was enacted not in 1865 but during the Eisenhower administration.

We're building the slums of 20 years hence.

... warning against building public housing projects in Nashville during the 1950s.

I would urge putting an end to the work being done on fire prevention. I don't know of anything I enjoy more than going to see a big fire, and reformers have no right to take this pleasure away from us citizens. The Health Department should also be eliminated. All this giving shots to prevent diseases has hurt the business of the National Casket Company severely. They are an old Nashville company with a big payroll, who pay large taxes, and what do we do with their tax money? -- we try to put them out of business.

... poking fun at reactionaries in Tennessee local government.

Never marry a man in uniform.

... implying that life in the armed services is so unpleasant that no soldier can make a rational decision on marriage.

Government regulations, either in war or in peace, are something like taxes or your wife's family. Nobody is in favor of them, yet it is pretty hard to get along without them.

Dramatic cures can be affected in individuals but never in groups.

Ah, the sixties. When Rome was in our condition, it took about four centuries for its final demise. Things move faster now, I fear.

I learned long ago that people who expect immediate economic miracles never majored in math at college.

~13~

Education

Some Kids Graduate Magna Cum Laude

"During the 1960s, there was a great deal of commotion on the Vanderbilt campus as the sexual revolution arrived at our conservative Southern school. I was called before the Board of Trustees, including May, and asked to explain our policy on introducing co-ed dorms.

"I had spent days carefully preparing my comments, and then spoke in serious tones for 30 minutes. I covered the three areas that kept young ladies virtuous: fear of hell-fire, fear of disease and the fear of pregnancy. When I was done, May stood up and said he could have saved me a lot of time and energy, and proceeded to recite this limerick:

There was a co-ed named Wilde,
Who kept herself quite undefiled,
By thinking of Jesus,
Contagious diseases,
And the trouble of having a child!

"That was Dan; he was absolutely amusing. But, more than that, he was smart. If you disagreed with him, you had better be informed, because Dan always knew what he was talking about when he took a stance."

- Dr. Alexander Heard, former chancellor, Vanderbilt University

"Some people's kids graduate from college *magna cum laude.* Mine graduated *"lawdy how come?"*
... also told with the ending, "... mine graduated cum fortuna."

Then there was the story about the professor who asked a young freshman, "What is electricity?" The student had not prepared his lesson, and in a stuttering voice said, "Professor, I knew, but I have forgotten."

The professor replied, "What a tragedy. For hundreds of years, men have tried to find how and what electricity is and you, a freshman, knew and forgot!"

Having a girlfriend in college is like carrying an extra course.

You can attend a Vanderbilt Board of Trust meeting, and you can park on the Vanderbilt campus, but you can't do both on the same day.

If a problem cannot be solved by education, it is insoluble.

I have no patience with the "edifice complex" of the education world. A great school system is not buildings, but strong teachers and a good curriculum.

There is nothing wrong with America's schools that a 100% increase in salary would not cure in 20 years. Paying poor teachers double would not improve their teaching, but it surely would get many better people to enter the profession.

A nation can be free or ignorant, but it cannot be both for very long.

That man knows a lot, but a lot of the stuff he knows ain't so.

I'll tell you how to spell "pneumonia." The "p" is silent, like in swimming.

I sat on the Vanderbilt University Board of Trust for 31 years, and received a steady flow of letters from anxious parents asking that I write a letter to the admissions office on behalf of their child. I would dutifully pen a thoughtful note to the admissions office about the student, and send a carbon copy to the thankful parents.

I had a little secret, however. Also on file at the admissions office was a letter I signed asking that all letters of recommendation from me be promptly ignored. And, apparently, they were.

Good students do not need references.

Dollars put wisely in good buildings, equipment, teachers and the training of students pay better dividends than other investments.

It does very little good to educate the geniuses if we cannot convince the masses.

The use of nouns for verbs like contact is unlimited. I hear some of my wife's friends say, "After I bridged this afternoon, I showered and then cocktailed at the club." Under the time-honored principles of "letting the punishment fit the crime," I believe these people should be grammared for life.

America's #1 problem: How to recruit strong teachers.

The primary purpose of schools is to educate, not to further any sociological concept.

If you copy from one man, it is plagiarism. If you copy from a dozen, it is research.

I am a great believer in basic education, as the making of a living is secondary to the making of a life.

Mathematics is pure logic, and there is no margin for error. All the fallacies found in the speeches of politicians and the blurbs of television, and even in sermons from the pulpit, have no place in this, the queen of all the sciences, mathematics.

Possibly the discovery of the number zero ranks with the invention of the wheel in the history of human progress.

I say the same thing at the Fisk board meeting in the morning and at the Vanderbilt board meeting at night. At Fisk, they think I'm a fascist and at Vanderbilt, they think I'm a communist.

... May sat simultaneously on the boards of Nashville's two leading centers of higher education – Fisk University, an all-black institution, and Vanderbilt University, known for its conservatism.

I sit on the boards of Vanderbilt University and Fisk University. I'm trying to drag one into the 20th century and the other back from the 21st.

I once heard a very brilliant educator say that being a quarterback on a college football team was the equivalent of any whole college year in giving a young man the understandings that are so necessary in life. I agree.

I recall the chat I once had with a groundskeeper at Vanderbilt University after one of the school's learned educators had been granted the title "Professor Emeritus."

The groundskeeper, who was very fond of the scholar, remarked, "He should of gotten that title 20 years ago."

Advice to college freshmen: Don't let the big shots get you down. All freshmen are just as green as you are, and possibly greener. They will all tell you how good they are, and this is human nature. A college freshman who wasn't a big wheel in high school is absolutely unknown.

~14~

Capitalism & Free Enterprise
Any Tinhorn Dictator Can Make the Rich Poor

"I was a Gentile and Dan was Jewish but there was no difference. Dan just saw a man.

"He always felt that he needed to contribute to the world. He'd always pick up trash, even if it wasn't his. Leave the world a better place than you found it; that was his way. I think I was first attracted to Dan because of his value system. And he had that tremendous breadth of interests. He lived outside himself. He was interested in all things, other than Dan May.

"I remember Dan invited me to lunch at the University Club with that group of his. Dan walked in with a suit, tie and tennis shoes. That gave me a good feeling. That's Dan May, secure in himself, not worrying what others will think.

"He was such a complicated man, but I took everything he told me at face value. You could bet your life what he said was true. And he always had those stories. I used to quote him in my Sunday School class."

- Morris Early, May's stockbroker

"Any tinhorn dictator can make the rich poor. Only free enterprise can make the poor rich.

Government grants don't cost anybody anything except for the taxpayers.

The Tennessee River flows through eight states and drains the other 40.

… in reference to the Tennessee Valley Authority, or T.V.A.
May maintained a lifelong skepticism about any enter-
prise or industry that was run by the government.

God pity the rich. The poor don't have to play golf or ride horseback.

Every Nashville millionaire either inherited it, married it, or is a little bit crooked.

Being rich doesn't make a man a fool; it merely gives him more
opportunity to show it.

My father is a marvelous example of a man who made a success out of himself by working hard. He came to this country with $7 in his pocket, and now he owes $50,000 to the bank.

All employees want profit-sharing. None wants loss- or even risk-sharing.

One of my fellow councilmen in Nashville once accused me of being a "rich S.O.B." I told him he was half right, but I was never going to tell him which half.

The low price that people put on freedom alarms me no end. The Robin Hood philosophy is very popular in the world today, but unfortunately, it always ends in the loss of personal freedom.

For a while, every dictatorship can steal from the well-to-do and give to the poor who are very happy to give up their freedom for this. Then, in a few years, the whole standard of living declines.

Industry is managed largely by people who have very little ownership, and labor is represented by people who haven't eaten out of a lunchbox in a generation.

American freedoms and all of our social programs come as a result of our great productivity. The Social Security program is wonderful, but India can't have one. If these great social gains could be accomplished by legislation, then all of South America could be prosperous by an act of their legislative bodies.

These great social aims are only possible in a free and competitive society, free from monopolies and other oppressors of production, irrespective of their social or economic status.

A very high percentage of the poor and ignorant refuse to pay the price necessary to escape their position. The price is hard work and a willingness to postpone present pleasures for future benefits. Obviously, those who don't want to improve themselves will not, no matter how many laws we pass or how many billions we spend. But there are some who have the desire and those we must help.

We planned one thing once, and that was Prohibition. It could have been made to work had we had a man to enforce it who combined the morals of Al Capone with the ruthlessness of Himmler and the executive organizational ability of Hitler. To make a planned economy work, it takes that.

The worst men always rise to the top in a planned economy.

I am a firm believer in the capitalistic system. In no other system yet devised have we discovered a *modus operandi* by which we can obtain as much economic well-being as expressed by the standard of living with a minimum of restraints on our civil and social liberties.

I'd be glad to support a guaranteed annual wage as long as the government also gives me a guaranteed annual profit.

The collective wisdom of almost all Americans is that our great nation owes a debt of gratitude to Labor for its diligence and dexterity, and that this wonderful land requires Capital to finance the buildings, machinery, tools, etc. for Labor to use.

Hence, each September we honor Labor with a holiday on the first Monday. I propose we pick a date, say the anniversary of the founding of the *The Wall Street Journal* or the New York Stock Exchange, to honor Capital, to be known as Corporation Day.

~15~

The May Family

"I began working at the May Hosiery Mills in the stock room in October 1933, at 15 cents an hour. When I retired 45 years later, I had worked with four generations of May men.

"I remember Dan May's father, Jake May, walking around the plant, talking to employees. But it was in 1937 that I started working in close contact with Dan May. He was a dollar-a-year man with the War Production Board during World War II.

"In April of 1944, Dan and I rode the train from Nashville to New York City. We left early in the morning on the L&N, and switched to the C&O to get to New York. Late in the afternoon, he turned to me and said, 'At this time of day, I always get homesick.' For Dan, the day's work was done and he wanted to go home to his family.

"I had access to Dan's office at the mill, and could walk in whenever I needed to talk to him. Once I went in there with some problem and he was talking to the cleaning lady. I began to tell him about whatever it was, and he cut me off. 'You wait your turn,' he said. 'This lady is just as important as you are.'"

- E.K. Walker, former production manager
of the May Hosiery Mills

"My brother has one thing I don't have...a hardworking brother.

None of them has ever done anything worth talking about.

… about his seven grandchildren.

114

After several decades of marriage, I can assure you that I make all the important decisions in this family...so far there haven't been any.

I've always thought about renting her out for the hunting season.

... on his wife's acute sense of smell.

My wife sent me to the grocery store for a head of lettuce soon after we were married. I came back with a head of cabbage, and was never sent to the grocery store again.

There's more pain in this world than pleasure.

... explaining his reluctance to have children.

May Hosiery Mills has a monopoly on hosiery worn on the moon.

...May Hosiery Mills was selected without solicitation by NASA to make the socks Neil Armstrong wore when man first stepped on the moon.

Any damn fool can make hosiery. It takes a genius to make money.

Then there was the time the receptionist at the May Hosiery Mills received a phone call from a Nashville city official. The caller wanted information on how many people worked at the mill, broken down by sex. The receptionist replied, "We ain't got none of those, but we do have a few broken down by alcohol."

My father always said the hosiery business was hell. He had a friend who was a minor executive with the L&N Railroad. My father would often cry to him about the hosiery business.

The railroad man said to my father one day, "You must have had a lot of money when you came down here to start that mill."

My father protested, "What made you think I had a lot of money? I came here with $6,000 and opened that mill!"

"Well, I've known you 20 years," the man replied. "You've been losing money every year, and you still have some left!"

I'm often asked how many people work at the May Hosiery Mills. The answer — About half of 'em!

The May Hosiery Mills slogan: You can't wear our socks out. You have to stay indoors!

The May Hosiery Mills motto: Second to none. Seconds to all!

They are on the sure side.

... referring to maternal ancestors.

I came home from work one spring day and said to my wife, "There's an article I want to read. Have you seen the May *Fortune?*"

She replied, "I've heard a lot about it, but I've never seen any of it!"

I may be a hero to some people but I am certain that I am nothing but an old fogey to my grandchildren. It is most difficult to fool a child!

I only knew one coward in the May family. It's my grandson Andy. He took one look at the family hosiery business and decided to enlist in a combat unit in the Marines.

May's Law #1: Anytime I write a letter to a man to remind him to pay me something, the check is there when I get home.

Have you heard about the new society on Wall Street called Apparel Anonymous? If you get the wild idea to purchase stock in an apparel company, you call them up and they talk you out of it.

My mother's family was poor but, like most German immigrants in New York City, they had a code of conduct which, although not perfect, had many characteristics which could be used in any age. Hard work was admired and the copy book maxims found in *Guffey's First Reader* were the rules they lived by. Family life was stressed and divorce was never thought of as an easy escape from the drudgery of family life.

My father, Jake May, had no use for *goniffs*, loafers, wasters, boozers, smokers (especially pipe smokers) and people who did not smile.
… 'Goniff' is Yiddish for cheater or thief.

Jake May detested waste of any kind – *"Nichts darf kaput gehen"* was his motto until he was very old. "Do without" was his creed, but, at the same time, don't neglect spending money for those things that were essential and important.

Healthful food, medical attention (there was little of that in my youth, God knows), respectable clothes, and charity, especially to help his fellow Jews and of course, the care of his family were the only items of expenditure he thought really worthwhile. Pleasures were all right, but only after adequate savings were squirrelled away.

... on his father. (Nichts darf kaput gehen is German for "Nothing should wear out.")

He was a man of whom you can be proud. He was an 'ole School Southerner, with all their virtues and shortcomings. Honest and polite, with a type of chivalry that bowed deeply to ladies but approved slavery. A code of conduct definitely ambivalent, but in its passing, we have all lost something of value.

... on his father-in-law, Jacob Fishel.

My daughter was married in a small ceremony in New York, and afterwards the wedding party met to celebrate at a private brunch. My son-in-law stood up to make the customary toast. He spoke for some time, and finally got around to thanking his in-laws for bringing his wife into the world.

I interrupted, "The pleasure was all mine!"

All of this business—announcements, rings, receptions, fancy clothing— is 99% *stush,* and I hope you remember that, irrespective of the importance some place on it.

... advising his daughter on marriage celebrations.
('Stush' is the Yiddish word for a lot of foolishness.)

~16~

Old World Aphorisms

Besser Wie in Hosen Gemacht

"The May family was responsible for getting some 210 Jews out of Germany in the years before World War II. I was a distant relative of theirs. Dan's role was secondary to his brother Mortimer. Mortimer came over to Germany in 1936, and promised me he'd get an affidavit. Dan was very supportive.

"I was just a few weeks short of my 17th birthday when I got to America in 1937. They were in a bind after they got us out. The Depression was on, and the Mays had to give an affidavit of support, not a promise of a job, because that would interfere with the unemployment problem. But Dan gave anyone of us who wanted a job at the May Hosiery Mills. I worked there, and so did my mother.

"A lot of us owe our lives to the Mays..."

- Ernest Freudenthal, retired Nashville textile executive

Dan May's father, Jacob May, was a German native who dotted his English speech with German expressions. Dan May used many of these expressions in his daily speech. A few of his favorites follow. Note a few have a word or two of Yiddish added.

"Besser wie in Hosen gemacht.

Literally: Better than doing it in your trousers.
Use: You expected a $500 order and got one for $200. Not much, but it's better than going to the bathroom in your pants.

Yuntav by the goyim.

Literally: A holiday for the non-Jews.
Use: Said of the gaudy decorations that appeared every year at Christmas time in
Nashville.

Der Apfel fallt nicht weit vom Stamm.

Literally: The apple does not fall far from the tree.
Use: Children don't differ much from their parents in their characteristics. If the
parents are second class, don't expect first class kids.

Immer etwas!
Literally: Always something!
Use: Life is one damn thing after another.

Hast im Kopf aber nicht im Bein.

Literally: Has in head but not in legs.
Use: The elderly have mental ideas about sex, travel and exercise, but are not able to
perform.

Was nicht ist revach.

Literally: What doesn't happen is profit.
Use: A cynical phrase. Don't expect good news. You didn't have a stroke today; evil
events that don't occur are the rewards of the day.

Alt und steif und dumm dazu.

Literally: Old and stupid on top of all these.
Use: Old age hits you in many places.

Auch ein mensch!

Literally: Also a man!
Use: You call that fellow a human being? (Pejorative)

Nur Gesund.
Literally: Only healthy.
Use: Nothing matters if you have your health.

Alt ist eine Krankheit.

Literally: Age is a disease.
Use: Age is a disease in itself; you don't have to have a specific problem.

Undank ist der welt lohn.

Literally: Ingratitude is the payment of the world.
Use: Ingratitude is the payment that mankind gives.

Komm ich nicht heute komm ich morgen.

Literally: If I don't come today, I'll come tomorrow.
Use: A laidback attitude, similar to the Spanish "manana."

Ausge lassen.

Literally: Frolicsome.
Use: To describe unruly behavior of kids or silly adults.

Aus gespielt.

Literally: Played out.
Use: To refer to individuals who are over the hill.

Schicker wie ein goy.
Literally: Drunk as a gentile.
Use: Drunk.

Mechulla ist trumpf.
Literally: Bankruptcy is trump.
Use: Broke is the order of the day. Said of a pretentious person who has no means.

Schon ist die jugend; sie kommt nie wieder.
Literally: Youth is wonderful; it will not return.
Use: Enjoy while you can.

Nicht nutz.
Literally: No use.
Use: A ne'er-do-well, but not so elegant as a ne'er-do-well. A bad actor.

State of Tennessee

THE SENATE

SENATE JOINT RESOLUTION NO. 15

IN MEMORY OF: DAN MAY, NASHVILLE–DAVIDSON
COUNTY BUSINESS AND CIVIC LEADER.

By Senator Douglas Henry, Jr.

WHEREAS, Dan May was born in Nashville on Christmas Day in 1898, and departed this life on December 16, 1982, during which eighty-three years he made Nashville his home and life and gave of himself in such fashion that this general assembly takes note thereof; and

WHEREAS, for thirty years he headed May Hosiery Mills, the first hosiery mill in the South which was founded in Nashville in 1896 by his father, Jacob May, a German immigrant; and

WHEREAS, he launched a career in local politics and education and established a reputation in the Nashville community for his keen insight and delightful wit; and

WHEREAS, through his many interests - government, business, education, politics, religion, he shared generously of his time, talent, and resources; and

WHEREAS, his service to the cause of education was never less than superior, he, having graduated from Vanderbilt University in 1919 and later served ten years on the Nashville Board of Education, thirty-one years on the Vanderbilt Board of Trust, nine years on the Fisk University Board of Trust, and having vigorously fought for adequate funding of his primary concern – public education; and

WHEREAS, his civic contributions included service as a member of the first Metro Council government, chairman of the Metro Action Commission, chairman of the Mid-Cumberland Comprehensive Health Council, president of the Nashville Rotary Club, editor of the Vanderbilt University newspaper, one of the founders of Zeta Beta Tau fraternity, and a member of the War Production Board during World War II; and

WHEREAS, he envisioned during his twelve year membership on the Davidson County Quarterly Court the Concept of a consolidated form of government for Nashville and Davidson County, and later was instrumental in translating this dream into reality and thus providing Nashville's Metro government as a model for other major metropolitan areas across the nation; and

WHEREAS, he was a devoted member and leader of The Temple and served as president of the Nashville Jewish Community Council; and

WHEREAS, through all his years and achievements he combined integrity and sense of civic duty with his serious concern and ever present humorous approach to life; now, therefore,

BE IT RESOLVED BY THE SENATE OF THE NINETY-THIRD GENERAL ASSEMBLY OF THE STATE OF TENNESSEE, THE HOUSE OF REPRESENTATIVES CONCURRING, That note is hereby taken of and acclaim hereby rendered to the exemplary life and the many varied works of excellence of the late Dan May.

BE IT FURTHER RESOLVED, That this general assembly does hereby express its appreciation for the solid contribution of Dan May to his city, county, state, and larger community.

BE IT FURTHER RESOLVED, That lives of such varied excellence are commended to be emulated by all Tennesseans, young and old.

BE IT FURTHER RESOLVED, That an appropriate copy of this resolution be transmitted to Mrs. Dorothy Fishel May and other members of the family, 4200 Harding Road, Nashville, Tennessee.

Adopted: February 14, 1983

SPEAKER OF THE SENATE

SPEAKER OF THE HOUSE OF REPRESENTATIVES

Lamar Alexander
GOVERNOR

124

～ Closing Thoughts ～

Dan May was born on Christmas day 1898, and died almost 84 years later on December 16, 1982. His dear friend, the former chancellor of Vanderbilt University, Harvie Branscomb, delivered his eulogy:

This is an occasion of sadness, but also of pride. We have lost much – in the head of a devoted and remarkable family, a rare friend for most of us in this room, a citizen who served us all with imagination, generosity and courage. We have lost much, and we share a many-sided sadness and grief. John Donne's oft-quoted words were never more appropriate: "Send not to ask for whom the bells toll; it tolls for (us)."

Dan May of all men, however, was not one who would wish to be enclosed in sorrow or overwhelmed by grief. Though the sadness abides and will continue, there is pride also, and happy memories, and gratitude that it has been our good fortune to have known and loved someone like Dan May.

I do not need to tell you of his achievements. They are written in the economy of this region, in the political structure of our community, in the work of many public service agencies and commissions, perhaps most of all in the educational institutions of our city. I prefer to take this opportunity to say a few words about Dan May as a person, as I knew him, and as most of you know him.

He was unique, combining in his temper and his mind qualities rarely found so vividly together. He owed this to many elements in his inheritance and his experience – to an Old World ancestry, to this great religious tradition in which he was reared, to his academic education, to the individuals who influenced him along the w way, and to the love, support and companionship of Dorothy Fishel May. But the real basis of his uniqueness was an inner strength and independence which enabled him to be and remain himself under all conditions and circumstances.

He was not a conformist. He could not be pressured into a course he did not believe in, nor seduced by the natural desire to be agreeable.

He said what he thought, and stood for what he believed in. Once, after he had been in a decided minority on an issue before a board on which he and I were members, he dismissed my reference to it with the remark he often used, "Don't forget that God and one are a majority." He laughed when he said it, but I knew him well enough to know that it expressed his character. Dan May had moral courage. He stood for what he believed. And he believed in the true and good. Dan didn't talk in those terms – he lived and thought in specific issues and problems, not in abstractions. I think that he would have agreed with William Blake's statement that "he who would do good to another must do it in particulars. General good," said Blake, "is the plea of hypocrites and the flatterers." But behind Dan's many specific issues and objectives lay a deep sense of fairness and human brotherhood. He was a champion of new opportunities for minorities and other underprivileged groups long before it was politically expedient to be so. He fought for schools that would be adequately supported and free from outside interference, with only the best education possible as the guiding principle. He worked tirelessly for better housing and better medical care for the blighted areas of our city. He served for many years as the Chairman of the School Board of Nashville, was on the Board of Fisk University for nearly a decade, and for 31 years served as a member of Vanderbilt's Board of Trust, rarely, if ever, missing a meeting, adopting at times unpopular positions, but standing always for the highest educational standards for his alma mater.

Dan May was a realist. He never confused good intentions with good results. The test was in the outcome. He knew the techniques and stratagems of political action, though he would not stoop to unethical methods to achieve a desirable end. I was associated with him once in an effort which he – and I – believed would represent a great improvement in an important public service. The issue came finally to depend on one man's vote and influence. "I knew that he could be persuaded," Dan told me, "by certain inducements. But if it had to be done that way," he continued, "we can do without the program." People differed with him from time to time, but they always trusted him. Though skillful in political action, and enjoying it, I think, he had no personal political ambitions. And yet, as has been said repeatedly in the last few days, probably no individual has had a greater influence for good on the life of this community than did Dan May.

Part of his realism was that he understood people and delighted in their foibles as well as in their virtues. I recall his remark on one occasion that "there is no man who became a scoundrel for $1,000 who would not have preferred to be an honest man for half the money." His wit was well-known, yet as Vanderbilt Chancellor Wyatt has commented, even on short acquaintance, it always had meaning. It carried a message. But it made him great company, and an evening with Dan May was for his friends an occasion of delight.

Understanding people, thus, and being free in his inner being and with great zest for living, Dan remained ever youthful in outlook and temper. "Nothing is invincibly young," wrote Santayana, "except spirit.... Old places and old persons when spirit dwells in them have an intrinsic vitality of which even youth is incapable." Dan May had that spirit and vitality. No one thought of him as old, though by the calendar it might be said to be true. He had that "balance of long perspective and wisdom" of which Santayana goes on to speak in the passage from which I have quoted. But Dan had something else – an imaginative and innovative spirit which is essentially youthful.

The greatest miracle of the universe is the human spirit, and we can be proud and grateful that we could know and work with Dan May. Let us thank God that he dwelt among us, and that we could love and rejoice in him.

Years ago I came across a quotation from one of your great teachers, which I have treasured, and which has come vividly to mind the last few days. Rabbi Tarphon said, "The day is short, and the task is great, and the Master of the House is urgent. It is not for thee to finish the work, nor art thou free to desist from it. And faithful is the Master of thy work."

☙ Acknowledgements ☙

M ANY THANKS TO each of the following. They all jogged their memories, making this book possible.

Delores Adams, Andrew Benedict, Harry S. Blum, Jr., Reba Blum, Robert Blum, Cawthon A. Bowen, Jr., Harvie Branscomb, Billy F. Bryant, Robert N. Buchanan, Jr., Bea Cohen, I.T. Creswell, Pearl Creswell, Frances H. Denney, Howard "Mack" Dobson, Frank W. Drowata, Winfield Dunn, Morris C. Early, Ann Eisenstein, Robert Eisenstein, Randall M. Falk, Frances Fishel, Sam Fleming, Ernest Freudenthal, Dianne Gilbert, Harris Gilbert, John Gilbert, Eleanor Glassman, Fred Goldner, Henry Goodpasture, Gus G. Halliburton, Charles W. Hawkins, Sr., Bruce Hawley, Alexander Heard, Hoyt G. Hill, Betty Hollender, Charles Howell III, Eli Jacobs, Ray A. Koch, Jack W. Kuhn, Herbert Levy, Robert E. Lillard, Claire Loventhal, Marion "May" Brown Lucas, M.I. Lusky, Robert Massie, Leon May, Robert McGaw, Bob McKeand, Whitson "Dutch" McLean, Ira L. Mendell, Ernest J. Moench, Richard M. Morin, Annette Morrison, William F. Moynihan, Eugene Pargh, Fitzgerald "Bud" Parker, Allen W. Pettus, Ann Pilsk, John W. Poindexter, Catherine Prince, Annette Levy Ratkin, Arthur Reed, Frank Ritter, Samuel S. Riven, Irv Ryerson, Shep Schwartz, Sylvan D. Schwartzman, John Seigenthaler, Jess Shaw, Herbert Shayne, Lou Silberman, Wilson Sims, Alden H. Smith, Blanche Stern, James Squires, Allen Sullivan, Robert C. Taylor, Joe Thompson, Molly Todd, Joe Torrence, E. Kinloch Walker, Lowe Watkins, Ron Watson, Betty Weesner, George Weesner, Lydia Weesner, Martha Weesner, Albert Werthan, Leah Rose Werthan, Mary Jane Werthan, Wayne Whitt, Madison Wiggenton, Ernest Williams III, Tandy W. Wilson III.

And to the staffs of:

– Special Collections and Archives, Jean and Alexander Heard Library, Vanderbilt University
– The University of Mississippi, Public Affairs Office
– Director of Special Collections, Fisk University Library
– The Tennessee State Library and Archives, Archives and Manuscripts Staff, notably Ann Alley, Robert DePriest, Wayne Moore and Catherine Prince
– The Archives of the Jewish Federation of Nashville and Middle Tennessee, with a

special thanks to Annette Levy Ratkin
– Vanderbilt University, News and Public Affairs
– *The Tennessean,* Library Staff
– Jewish Federation, *The Observer*
– The Rotary Club of Nashville

I am indebted to a wonderful collection of old friends who provided support and advice along the way, especially Margaret Charles Brault, Rebecca Chetham, Jeffrey Sutton and Margaret Southard Sutton.

Matthew Lynch designed the book, and handled my constant nitpicking with grace and dignity. Much appreciated for all, Matt.

Every one of Dan May's descendents was indispensable in putting this book together. My thanks to his other six grandchildren, whose memories of grandpa proved invaluable: Maria May, Josh May, Andy May, Ben May, David May Stern and Sarah May Stern. The unconditional support and love of my mom and dad, Elizabeth "Boopie" May Stern and Walter P. Stern, was everpresent, as always. Uncle Joseph "Jack" May gave up countless weekends teaching me about Dan May and life. He deserves a book of his own sayings. Jack's late wife, Natalie McCuaig May, picked up on a passing comment of mine (when she was already quite sick), and encouraged me to write the book. She was a daily inspiration to me, and to all who knew her. And my grandma, Dorothy Fishel May, is no doubt embarrassed about all the fuss. Grandpa used to say she was "the only perfect person I know." I now see why. Thanks for all, Grandma.

∾ About the Author ∾

William "Willy" May Stern is the fourth of Dan and Dorothy May's seven grandchildren. He is a Chicago correspondent for Forbes.

Previously, he worked as a journalist in the United States, New Zealand, South Africa and Japan.

Stern was educated at Williams College and Harvard University, but learned most of what he knows at home.

Printed by Vanderbilt University Printing Services, Nashville, Tennessee